Powerboat Race

by Stephen Rickard

Published by Ransom Publishing Ltd.
51 Southgate Street, Winchester, Hampshire SO23 9EH
www.ransom.co.uk

ISBN   978 184167 786 6

First published in 2010

A CIP catalogue record of this book is available from the British Library.

The right of Stephen Rickard to be identified as the author of this Work has been
asserted by him in accordance with sections 77 and 78 of the Copyright, Design and
Patents Act 1988.

LIFE AT THE EDGE

POWERBOAT RACE

STEPHEN RICKARD

Ransom

Main engines.
There are two.

Hatch.
To get into the cockpit.

Propellors.
There are two. They turn up
to 66 times every second.

EVOLUTION P1 POWERBOAT

Hull.
Made of carbon fibre.

Cockpit.
Two seats – for the throttle man
and driver.

POWERBOAT DATA

Length:	12.3 metres
Height:	2.0 metres
Engines:	Two. 750 bhp each
Top speed:	193 km/hour (120 mph)

Hi. My name is Nigel Hook.
I race offshore powerboats.

That's my job.

I race P1 Evolution class
powerboats. They are fast.

They are so fast that you
need two pilots in each boat.

Today is race day. It is a Powerboat P1 Grand Prix.

At a race, we have two pits.

These are the dry pits. They are on land.

This is our race boat. It is called the Skater V399.

It is very heavy. It weighs more than 5,000 kg.

We use a big crane to lift it into the water.

Can you see the propellors?

The boat has two engines and two propellors.

Each engine gives 750 horse power.

This boat is three times more powerful than a Ferrari.

There is no speed limit in a Powerboat P1 Grand Prix race.

Now the boat is in the water.

Shelley checks the engine with the team.

This is the last check before the race.

Shelley is the first woman driver in Evolution powerboat racing.

It's just before the race. She is doing an interview for TV.

Then it's back to work.

Shelley and I think about the race.

How will we win?

All the powerboats head out to the start line.

Lots of other boats come with us.

The race will begin soon.

We are travelling at 115 mph. This is nearly top speed.

The waves make it very bumpy – and very dangerous. My body begins to hurt.

We must be careful too. The boat might roll over.

It's a good job we are strapped in.

The fans watch from the shore. They get to see everything.

We think hard about the race. Shelley steers the boat. I decide how fast to go.

There are no brakes.

We work as a team.

It is very loud in the cockpit.

We have radios in our helmets.

This is so we can talk to each other during the race.

We pass a marker on the course. Now we must turn hard.

We are in third place.

I'm having a fantastic time. But I don't have time to think about how much fun it is.

I must focus.

I hear the team yelling on the radio.

Everybody is very happy.

I want to hug Shelley. But I can't – we are both strapped in!

So we just hi-five. And laugh like crazy.

It is a great feeling to win a Powerboat P1 Grand Prix.

I am very tired and my bum is sore. But a win like this is not something to forget.

We are a great team!

WORLD CHAMPIONSHIP

Jargon Buster

autograph
brake horse power (bhp)
carbon fibre
cockpit
concentrate
course
driver
engine bay
Evolution
Grand Prix

hatch
helmet
interview
lap
offshore
P1
pilot
powerboat
propellor
radio
throttle man